FOREWORD

by the Rt. Rev. Cyril Bowles Lord Bi

G000277741

The county and diocese of Derby, which cover almost precisely the same area within very nearly the same boundaries, have in them very large stretches of some of the most beautiful countryside in England. They are most delightfully varied and the impression is none the less pleasing because the transition from one type of scenery to another is sometimes abrupt. It is surprising that a large part of the population of the country, including people who know and love other areas of natural beauty, is ignorant of the loveliness of Derbyshire.

There is the same surprising ignorance about our churches. This is to be found not only in people who do not know the county but also in those who visit it and even in some who live in it. It is sad that this should be so because a great many of our Derbyshire churches form part of our national architectural heritage. Their styles span the centuries. Tombs and monuments tell our history in other ways. There is fine local craftsmanship in stone, wood and metal. Their exteriors mostly unite the loveliness of scenery and building, of tree and spire or tower. Their interiors, lovely in themselves, have the additional attractiveness produced by devoted care over the years and reverent worship in the past and the present. As with our scenery, there are abrupt transitions which are very pleasing. To take one striking example, our Cathedral of All Saints, Derby, little known and foolishly neglected by visitors, moves with grace from its superbly proportioned and decorated early sixteenth century tower to its splendidly austere and dignified early eighteenth century nave and aisles.

We have, of course, our nineteenth century churches built to serve those who came to work, or were born to work, in our mills and mines and heavy industries. Some of these churches may seem to match the hardness of the work of these people and the bleakness of their surroundings, but some of them have their own fascinating style and their own distinctive character. They record a vital phase, whose influence is still with us, of the history of England and its national Church. We also have our little churches among the hills where for generations the struggle for existence was severe and where contact with the cultured world outside was much restricted. In these

churches and   nd alterations made to them, is the life-story of local communities mostly engaged in farming or quarrying. For each of them its parish church was a treasury into which, like the poor widow observed by Our Lord, it poured all its living.

Here are described some of the finest buildings of our county and diocese. They are only some of them. May this text and these pictures encourage many to explore and observe, learn and worship in the buildings they describe and in others of our treasures.

Front cover : The Norman nave of Melbourne Church (see page 15).

Opposite : St. Wystan's Crypt, Repton is one of the most important Saxon survivals in England. Beautiful in its simplicity, it was filled in and forgotten for centuries until it was cleared out and restored at the beginning of the last century (see page 17).

Right : This fine representation of the Royal Arms of George II surmounting Bakewell's magnificent screen in Derby Cathedral is a reminder that the Sovereign is Head of the Anglican Church.

The spire of St. Oswald's rises to 212 feet.

ASHBOURNE— *St. Oswald*

The present building was dedicated in 1241 and its lofty spire, 212 feet in height, dates from the 14th century though undoubtedly a Saxon church of modest dimensions once occupied the site, and remains of a Norman crypt have been identified.

There is a strange feeling of asymmetry as one enters the church and this is because there is no north aisle.

The interior is full of interest, the main glories being the East Window and the monuments. The Perpendicular East Window is filled with Victorian stained glass by Kempe, one of the best craftsmen in this medium of the 19th century.

In the Boothby Chapel is a splendid series of monuments representing the heads of the Cockayne family from 1372 to 1592. They are all there in marble or brass with the exception of one, Thomas Cockayne, who lies in Youlgrave Church (q.v.).

The great East Window with glass by Kempe.

Right: Medieval painted wooden panels in the Boothby Chapel.

Left: The 19th century pulpit has bluejohn inlays.

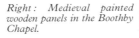

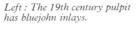

Penelope Boothby's famous monument.

There are many other monuments, to the Boothby family and others, but the one which has the greatest human appeal is the recumbent child sculptured to the memory of Penelope Boothby, the young daughter of Sir Brooke and Lady Boothby of Ashbourne Hall. Penelope was their only child and died aged 5 in 1791. Thomas Banks, R.A., wrought this moving memorial which was to bring him considerable fame.

Above: Wall monument to Sir John Manners (d.1584) and his wife Dorothy Vernon.

Left: Monument to Sir Godfrey and Lady Foljambe carved 1385.

Right: Saxon and Norman masonry in the porch.

BAKEWELL— *All Saints*

The church stands well above the small town, its unusual octagonal tower and battlemented walls making an interesting profile against the sky. Fragments of Saxon and Norman work preserved indicate a much older predecessor to the present building and an early 9th century Saxon cross stands in the churchyard. The main church dates from the 12th and 13th centuries with 19th century restorations.

This was the parish church used by the Vernons and Manners of Haddon Hall and their monuments are among the most interesting features of the building. Here lie Sir George Vernon, 'King of the Peak', and his daughter and son-in-law Dorothy Vernon and John Manners. Other interesting points to note are the exceptionally interesting and beautiful 14th century wall figures commemorating Sir Godfrey and Lady Foljambe and the early 14th century font which is particularly fine.

BOLSOVER –

St. Mary and St. Laurence

This fine church survives in spite of two disastrous fires, one in 1897 and the other in 1960. It is to the credit of all concerned that on both occasions the building was completely restored.

The main interest within, apart from the beautifully restored appearance of the church, is the Cavendish Chapel which miraculously escaped damage in both fires. Two colossal monuments face each other in this Chapel added in 1624. The older one is to Sir Charles Cavendish, Bess of Hardwick's third son and his wife, Baroness Ogle. It is a sumptuous creation with recumbent and kneeling figures. Opposite is a very different memorial – that to Sir Charles's grandson the 2nd Duke of Newcastle. It was designed by James Gibbs in strictly Palladian form – a huge pediment supported by corinthian columns around a black marble sarcophagus. The Duke died in 1691 but the monument was not erected until 1727 by his granddaughter the Countess of Oxford.

There are other monuments to the Cavendish family and their descendants the Bentincks who between them have been associated with Bolsover's Castle and Church since the early 17th century.

In spite of the faith in the future exhibited by the rebuildings, the church is still at risk – and by a far more insidious threat than fire. The extensive coalmining around has caused cracks to appear in the fabric. This also happened to the Castle, though that has now been remedied.

Monument to the 2nd Duke of Newcastle.   *View of the nave looking east.*   *Memorial to Sir Charles Cavendish.*

CHESTERFIELD—
Our Lady and All Saints

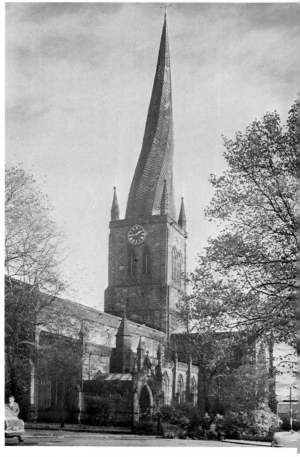

Even if it were not for the twisted spire – one of the most famous landmarks in England – the important parish church of Chesterfield, the largest in the county, would be notable in its own right.

Most of the nave and tower date from the early 14th century but the central piers, transepts and eastern chapels are as early as 1234. Gilbert Scott made a sympathetic restoration of the building around 1843 and his mark is left most notably in the Chancel window, the west door and the west gallery. He removed the box pews and some of the older galleries.

The church contains a number of chapels, a reminder of the many rich trade guilds which abounded in Chesterfield long ago. These chapels which they endowed are a sign both of their piety and their wealth.

The church is rich in screens and stained glass, some of the latter being modern; i.e. the work of Christopher Webb in the East Window and that of one of the greatest 20th century ecclesiastical architects, the late Sir Ninian Comper.

An important feature of the church is the Lady Chapel, sometimes known as the Foljambe Chapel because of the many alabaster monuments to that family which fill it.

One of the great treasures of the church was the Schnetzler organ, dating from 1756, which had been thoroughly restored and was in regular use.

Above: After Salisbury England's most celebrate spire.

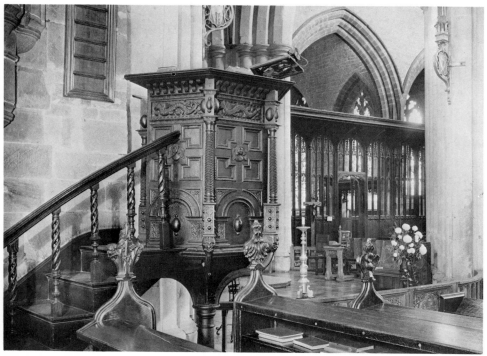

The pulpit is Jacobean and the carved screen dates from the early 16th century.

The High Altar and East Window with the Webb glass. To the right is the Lady Chapel.

Below right : The 15th century processional cross ; a rare pre-Reformation treasure.

Unfortunately, the fire of 1961 which swept through this part of the building, completely destroyed it. Now the North Transept holds a vast and very fine replacement, the rebuilt Lewis organ which came from Glasgow City Hall and now incorporates all the surviving stops from the old instrument.

A treasure which, happily, was not affected by the fire is the magnificent late 15th century processional cross, illustrated here.

But for all the magnificence within and the great historical significance of this church, its greatest popular appeal will always be the result of what may have been the faulty judgment of some long-dead craftsmen – the twisted spire. The great affection felt throughout the Midlands for this church is as much for this imperfection as for its great qualities.

A few statistics will answer the questions of the curious: the spire is 228 feet in height with eight flat surfaces. It leans $9'\ 4\frac{3}{8}''$ to the south-west, $8'\ 6\frac{7}{8}''$ to the south and $3'\ 9\frac{3}{8}''$ to the west.

Below : St. Catherine's Chapel with its medieval wood screen.

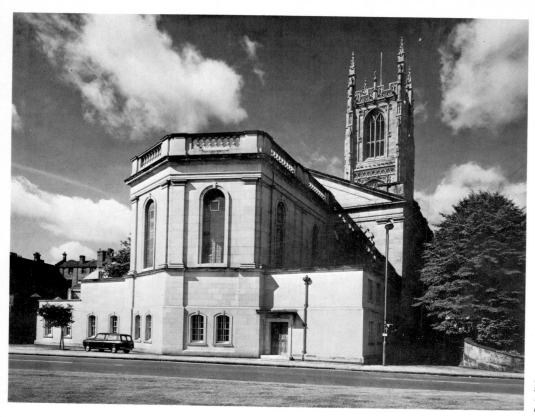

All Saints from the north east showing Sebastian Comper's extension.

DERBY– *The Cathedral of All Saints*

At the beginning of the 18th century, apart from its magnificent tower, there was nothing particularly remarkable about the old Parish Church of Derby, then a small, quiet market town except that it was very dilapidated. In fact by 1723 the structure was unsafe and in spite of being prevented by the 18th century equivalent of red tape from doing anything about it, the courageous incumbent of the time, the Rev. Dr. Michael Hutchinson, ordered the entire structure, except the tower, to be pulled down in the small hours of February 18th. The deed was done and no doubt there was an outcry, but soon designs were accepted from James Gibbs for the rebuilding, which is virtually as we see it today. Gibbs was the designer of many distinguished churches including St. Martin's-in-the-Fields, perhaps his most famous work.

Working in association with Gibbs was Francis Smith ('Smith of Warwick' as he is usually known) and the great ironsmith Robert Bakewell whose screen is one of the most notable features of the interior.

Some relics of the old church survive, notably Bess of Hardwick's great monument which was erected in her own lifetime.

In 1970 the interior was dingy and depressing but by the Spring of 1972 it had all been restored to its Georgian splendour with some notable new additions including the huge baldachino over the altar.

Ponsonby monuments by Rysbrack and Nollekens.

8

A new extension at the east was also completed to the designs of Mr. Sebastian Comper, son of the great Sir Ninian Comper.

In 1974 the grime of centuries was removed during the cleaning of the tower so that now Derby Cathedral (Derby having been formed into a diocese in 1927) is one of the most splendid 18th century churches in England.

There are numerous interesting wall monuments including one by Sir Francis Chantrey and another designed by James Gibbs, a commission he no doubt accepted while supervising the rebuilding work. The more patrician monuments to the Ponsonby family, Earls of Bessborough, who were closely related to the Devonshire family, are notable objects in the Cavendish aisle and they have recently been cleaned as has Bess of Hardwick's. The Cavendish Vault is now a chapel.

Another interesting and poignant object is the Jacobite tablet erected in 1945 to commemorate the bicentenary of the last Jacobite Rising of 1745 and the arrival of Prince Charles Edward Stuart in Derby at the head of the Highland army. The Prince attended devotions in the church which would have been as fresh and new looking then as it is today.

Apart from the new structural additions the 20th century is well represented by wrought ironwork and the two east windows in the aisles which are filled with stained glass of modern design by Ceri Richards.

Most of the bells were recast in the 17th century but the tenor bell is well over 500 years old. The parish registers date from 1558.

ELVASTON –

St. Bartholomew

Although the parish church of Elvaston and district, St Bartholomew's stands aloof from the village and close to the great Castle as if it were the private chapel of the Earl of Harrington who lived there until fairly recently, and whose monuments are such a feature of the building.

This large, handsome church dates in part from the 1200s but it is mainly of later work with restorations and extensions by G. F. Bodley in the 1900s. Notable among these embellishments is the carved reredos in the Sanctuary – a memorable example of early nineteenth century craftsmanship. Bodley, like Pugin, gave to his churches and restorations an atmosphere of Tractarian catholicity well exemplified at Elvaston.

Most of the best monuments are to the Stanhopes including a massive one to Sir John (d. 1610) and Lady Stanhope and a semi-recumbent armoured figure of Sir John Stanhope (d. 1648), brother of the 1st Earl of Chesterfield. The 5th Earl of Harrington is represented by a very fine marble recumbent effigy, upon the tomb-chest of which we read that he died in 1862 and was with Byron in Greece. Perhaps the gem of the church is the large wall tablet to the third Earl carved by Canova and said to be one of only three in England by that distinguished sculptor.

Left : The fine Perpendicular tower.

Below left : Canova's monument to the 3rd Earl of Harrington.

Below : The 1905 reredos in the Sanctuary.

Below right : Monument to Sir John and Lady Stanhope.

EYAM—

St. Laurence

The architectural merits of this 13th century church with its restorations by G. S. Street is somewhat overshadowed by the Great Plague connexions and the gallant vicar, William Mompesson, whose chair is in the church and whose wife is buried in the churchyard.

The building is notable for the size of its chancel – almost as big as the nave. This was re-built and presumably extended in the 1600s. There are some interesting wall paintings and early incised slabs. Apart from the famous Saxon cross the churchyard contains numerous fine tombstones *in situ* including one to Richard Furniss, Eyam's own poet.

The Saxon font and Saxon cross remind us that there has been Christian worship here for well over a thousand years.

Left: One of the best preserved Saxon crosses in England.

Below left: The crude Saxon font.

Below: Tomb-chest of Mrs. Mompesson.

HARTINGTON— *St. Giles*

The village of Hartington is in one of the most beautiful, and therefore popular, areas of Derbyshire. The Perpendicular west tower of its cruciform, battlemented church is a landmark in the village and the old building stands surrounded, as it should be, with the fine old headstones marking where 'the rude forefathers of the hamlet sleep'.

The impression on entering the building is of width and space. Pevsner points out several aspects of similarity in detail with St. Mary's, Wirksworth notably the arcades between nave and aisles. Items of interest to note are the fragments of early wall paintings, the old parish chest, a gauntlet (probably for ceremonial use at some stately funeral of long ago) and the 'Patriarchs of Israel' – a series of early eighteenth century painted panels.

There is an effigy of a woman, thought to represent a thirteenth century Countess of Derby of the de Ferrers family, who was Lady of the Manor. She holds a heart in her hand.

The bulk of the building dates from the early 13th century with improvements in the next. By the mid-19th century St. Giles, as with so many churches of similar age, was in need of an overhaul. This was carried out in 1858. Some buildings were changed for the worse and some even ended up beyond recognition. The restoration of the church at Hartington, however, was done with some sensitivity and, given the date, came out of it luckier than many.

Above : The battlemented exterior set amongst the tombstones.

Left : A glimpse of the South Transept showing some of the 'Patriarchs of Israel' panels and the gauntlet.

HATHERSAGE — *St. Michael*

Hathersage is in the country of the Eyre family and their arms adorn the porch of the church and their brasses are a feature of the interior. Both church and village have strong links with Charlotte Brontë. St. Michael's stands high above the village with a notable perpendicular tower. The E. window glass is interesting not only because it is the work of Kempe but also because it came from the submerged church at Derwent now beneath the reservoir.

The glass was put here in 1949, salvaged from the church.

Charlotte Brontë stayed in the vicarage with her friend Ellen Nussey and derived inspiration from local houses and families for her novel 'Jane Eyre'. Even the name was taken from the family whose brasses are illustrated below.

Visitors look with astonishment at the freakishly long, railed grave of Robin Hood's friend 'Little John' who is alleged to lie beneath.

The reputed grave of 'Little John'.

Eyre brasses in the Sanctuary.

KEDLESTON—
All Saints

The church is closely enfolded to the north and east by Kedleston Hall

The church is all that remains of old Kedleston village, swept away by the 1st Lord Scarsdale. It stands as an adjunct to the great house, a pious medieval foil to the Age of Reason. The building contains many memorials to the Curzon family, the earliest being Richard de Curzon, a 13th century Lord of the Manor and ending with the late 2nd Viscount Scarsdale. The most sumptuous memorial is that to Marquess Curzon of Kedleston and his first wife,

uncle of the late and of the present Lord Scarsdale. Curzon restored the church and added the North Aisle to the designs of the great Victorian architect G. F. Bodley in 1907. The wrought iron is very fine and the whole concept that of an 18th century magnate rather than a 20th century statesman.

The south doorway is Norman but the main structure is late 13th century. Apart from the monuments, there are other items of interest to be seen, notably the Curzon standard – a rare survival, and the beautiful hatchment to the 2nd Lord Scarsdale's first wife, Sophia Noel, who was a co-heiress of the barony of Wentworth and aunt to Lady Byron wife of the poet.

Left : The nave showing two of the Scarsdale hatchments.

Below : The Curzon aisle built by Marquess Curzon to accommodate his own and his first wife's recumbent effigies, just visible through the wrought iron.

MELBOURNE—
St. Michael with St. Mary

Henry Thorold in his account of Melbourne church describes it as 'numinous' – infused with divinity – and this is a most effective description of what is one of the finest Norman parish churches in England. Most of the building is 12th century and the tall rounded piers of the nave are four feet in diameter and make an impressive sight on entering, rather like a miniature Norwich or Durham.

No other parish church of this date has a two-towered west facade.

One reason for the size and importance of this church in a relatively small community was that the previous church was granted to the Bishops of Carlisle by Henry I in 1133 together with the manor. As a result of the increased raids

Romanesque carving on the capitals.

on England made by the Scots, Carlisle became a dangerous place; the Bishop moved his court to Melbourne, and rebuilt the church in a style fit for a Bishop.

The pillars of the East tower arch each have elaborately decorated capitals, the fine carving being reminiscent of the basilica of Vezelay in Burgundy.

The church has been altered considerably over the years. The tower was made higher in 1602 and the roof-line was lowered in the 18th or early 19th centuries (easily seen from the exterior), so that it must have been at one time even more impressive. However, in spite of this the church retains the essentially powerful impact which only this type of Norman building can make.

The building is unique in two respects – its two-towered west facade and its triple narthex.

View from the south east.

NORBURY
St. Mary
with
St. Barlock

Left : The south door and tower.

Right : The Chancel.

Below : Monument to Ralph and Elizabeth Fitzherbert, 1491. Early 14th century glass.

Below right : Palimpsest brass to Sir Anthony and Lady Fitzherbert.

A noble building of modest proportions, Norbury church stands in superb surroundings close to Norbury Manor, a Queen Anne house, and the 13th century Hall-house of the Fitzherberts, forming an interesting group. This church is remarkable for the size of its chancel relative to the rest of it, being scarcely three feet shorter than the nave. It is the resting place of several Fitzherberts whose presence in stone, alabaster and brass dominates the whole church.

Henry Kniveton, a 14th century rector of Norbury, built the chancel, but the north aisle of the nave and the chapels east and west of the tower and the tower itself were built by members of the Fitzherbert family in the 15th and 16th centuries.

In the late 12th century a John Fitzherbert was governor of Waterford which is said to account for the unusual dedication to St. Barlock, an Irish saint.

Much of the glass is pre-Reformation and is undergoing the lengthy process of being cleaned and restored. The Lady Chapel windows (c.1465) have already been restored by York Minster craftsmen.

The brass to Sir Anthony Fitzherbert and his family is notable. Apart from being a fine brass in itself

it is interesting in as much as the figure of Sir Anthony himself, a lawyer and Justice of the Common Pleas, is 'second-hand' (i.e. a palimpsest), having been taken from Croxden Abbey, Uttoxeter at the time of the Dissolution. It formerly represented one Matilda de Verdun, but was reversed and used again. As the shape was that of a woman, Sir Anthony was cunningly represented in his lawyer's robes.

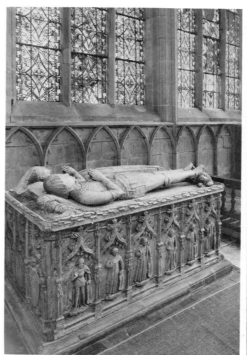

REPTON—
St. Wystan

St. Wystan's magnificent timber roof with its carved foliated bosses.

There are reliable contemporary records to prove the burial of King Ethelbert of Mercia in Repton in 757 and the existence of a monastery (and therefore a church) at least sixty years earlier; yet on this evidence alone such early dates could not be claimed for any of the present buildings. Nor do later records of the burial of King Wiglaf in 840 or St. Wystan in 850 by themselves justify any similar claim. But recent studies, especially excavations still in progress in 1980, have established that the eastern part of the church was standing when the great army of the Danes wintered in Repton in 874-5. Thus the crypt can now confidently be identified not only as the mausoleum of King Wiglaf but also as the place where pilgrims venerated the relics of his grandson St. Wystan to whom the church is dedicated.

The later medieval nave and tower, mainly of the fourteenth and fifteenth centuries, are also worthy of careful study; as are the interesting monuments, including one of alabaster beside the north entrance to the crypt.

The south elevation of Repton Church.

STEETLEY CHAPEL

This is Derbyshire's answer to Scotland's Rosslyn Chapel. Once used as a cowshed and later roofless and overgrown it was rescued in the 1870s and restored by the distinguished Victorian architect J. L. Pearson. In 1880 the building was re-consecrated by the Bishop of Lichfield.

Its near identical twin is Kilpeck, Herefordshire, but otherwise a rarity – this tiny masterpiece of Norman architecture with its carved embellishments standing aloof from human habitation some distance from the village of Whitwell. It is a bit of a mystery, too, as the original purpose of building such a place of worship has never been satisfactorily settled. It looks as if it were once the private chapel of some great family, but history is silent on the subject.

At its maximum dimensions, Steetley Chapel measures but 52 feet in length by 15 feet in width and consists of an aisleless nave, a square chancel and groin-vaulted apse. Pearson took the oppor-

tunity of adding his own embellishments during the restoration so that some of the features are Victorian rather than Norman, but none the less interesting for that. The most notable addition made by the architect was the addition of pediment over the richly decorated south door. This is in the form of what is almost a right-angled triangle with reticulated decorations and cross motifs.

The chancel arch has elaborately carved triple mouldings resting on capitals carved to depict Adam and Eve, St. George and other subjects. The whole building is lit by narrow rounded-top windows.

During the restoration a carved stone was found bearing Celtic crosses and symbols of the Mass. One theory is that this stone was a monument to Lawrence de Leche, a priest who officiated here during the Black Death.

Above: The apse showing carved Norman capitals.

Steetley from the east. Notice the elaborately decorated string course and the carved corbels.

TIDESWELL—
St. John the Baptist

St. John the Baptist was built entirely in the 14th century and is therefore an interesting specimen of pure Decorated architecture combined with some Perpendicular features and though only a parish church, its overall magnificence has earned it the popular description of "The Cathedral of the Peak".

The interior is no less grand and cathedral-like. Entering from the West the graceful and lofty arches draw the eye upwards to the open timbered roof and eastwards towards the great window with its fine Victorian stained glass depicting the Tree of Jesse designed by C. G. S. Foljambe whose own forbears were benefactors of the church centuries before.

The choirstalls have some rich carving as well as misericord seats and the fine carved chancel screen is original.

In the middle of the Chancel floor is a large tombchest to Sir Sampson Meverell in Purbeck marble. Sir Sampson was a veteran of the Hundred Years' War and fought in 12 battles in France. The incised crosses on the top of the tomb indicate that it was at one time used as an altar.

There are two Chantry Chapels in the south Transept – the de Bower Chapel and the Lytton Chapel, both containing monuments to these families, the latter being forbears of the Lyttons of Knebworth in Hertfordshire.

Elsewhere are brasses to Bishop Pursglove shown in pre-Reformation mass vestments although he died in 1579 (he refused the Oath of Supremecy in 1559) and to members of the Foljambe family. One brass to John Foljambe who died in 1383 has a Latin inscription saying that he provided many good things for the building of the church.

WIRKSWORTH—

St. Mary the Virgin

Although the great grey Church of St. Mary the Virgin gives off an aura of dim timelessness and mystery, it has been the subject of some rigorous restoration in the last century starting in the 1820s some decades before the most devastating wave of restorations of the pious but sometimes insensitive Victorians. That age, too, left its mark with further alterations in 1855 and finally it was lucky enough to have the attentions of Sir George Gilbert Scott in the 1870s.

The earliest parts of the building date from 1272 but some fragments of Saxon and Norman stonework which have been preserved are survivors of an earlier church. One carved stone is particularly interesting. It shows a king, seated and crowned and wearing a moustache, with his hand on his heart as if he were taking an oath. He is looking at a figure which might be his queen or a bishop giving blessing. This figure is dressed in a curious heart-shaped stomacher and has one crudely-carved hand raised.

Most of the present building dates from the 13th, 14th and 15th centuries and is part Perpendicular and part Decorated but the evidence of a more distant past is ever present, especially when one sees the Wirksworth Stone – the purpose of which is obscure but which probably marked the grave of Betti, the traditional founder of the church (A.D. 653) illustrating scenes from the life of Christ in the characteristically crude but beautiful sculptured style

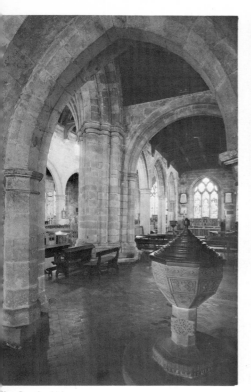

The South Aisle.

Above right: Fragments from an earlier church including the carving of a king and queen or bishop.

Right: The Wirksworth Stone showing scenes from the life of Christ.

Left: Gell monuments.

of the eighth century. The scenes depicted are: Washing the Disciples' feet, Cross with a lamb, Symbols of the four Evangelists, The burial of the Blessed Virgin, The Descent into Hell, The Ascension, The Annunciation and a final scene that has been variously interpreted.

Another notable feature is the large 12th century font standing on four sturdy romanesque legs. It was obviously used for total immersion. There is another font dating from the 17th century.

Two major local families are the Blackwalls and the Gells. Their monuments are to be seen here dating back to the early 15th century including an incised slab and a fine alabaster effigy representing Ralph and Anthony Gell respectively. Both families are still very much connected with town and church.

Another interesting monument is one to Anthony Lowe who died in 1583 and who personally served four sovereigns. The monument has been restored to its original colouring.

21

YOULGRAVE—
All Saints

The tall, broad tower of this church, one of the most impressive in Derbyshire, is a striking feature of the village, thrusting itself forward and upwards to dominate the street. The exterior is mainly Perpendicular though the nave pillars are late Norman as is the font – the only one in England with a stoup attached.

The chancel is particularly impressive with the tomb of Thomas Cockayne in the centre. This fine 15th century knightly effigy is the 'missing' one from the series of Cockayne monuments in Ashbourne Church (see page 2). It is only three feet six inches in length, probably because Thomas died before his father in a fight on the way to Tamworth Church in 1488. He wears Yorkist emblems and under his head is the Cockayne crest – a cock's head, probably a piece of punning heraldry. There are other interesting monuments and an attractive brass of 1603.

The East window, predominantly an unusual copper hue, was designed by Sir Edward Burne-Jones and made by William Morris's firm. Other windows in the north aisle and the nave have the distinctive characteristics of the work of Charles Eamer Kempe.

A side chapel in the north aisle was dedicated to King Charles the Martyr through the office of the late Captain H. S. Wheatly-Crowe, dedicated Royalist and protagonist of the Martyr King.

The High Altar, Burne-Jones windows and monument to Thomas Cockayne.

The church and churchyard from the south east.

OTHER CHURCHES IN BRIEF

Right: St. Edmund's, Castleton, of ancient origin but much rebuilt in 1837. There is, however, a fine Norman chancel arch and all the 17th century box pews are intact. An unusual feature is the library, left by a former incumbent in 1817 for the benefit of parishioners, consisting of some 200 volumes housed in the church.

Below: The Chapel of St. John the Baptist, Matlock Bath, a chapel-of-ease with high-church origins built in 1897 to the designs of Sir Guy Dawber.

Below right: St. John the Baptist, Buxton – a late Georgian Italianate church with rich 19th century embellishments.

Left: 15th century chapel at Haddon Hall. Note St. Christopher amongst the wall murals and part of the beautiful monument to Lord Haddon designed by his mother, Violet Duchess of Rutland.

Above: Unusual wall-monument in Eckington Church to George and Margaret Sitwell, of Renishaw.

Below left: St. Giles, Marston Montgomery has an unusual bellcote.

Below: The beautiful Edwardian lectern in All Saints, Mackworth.